DATABASE OF
RENDERING PROTOCOLS

DATABASE OF RENDERING PROTOCOLS

PARIS TOSEN

Tosen Books

Database of Rendering Protocols

Second Edition, 2011

ISBN 978-1-926949-11-6

Cover and book design by Paris Tosen

www.tosenbooks.ca

Contents

The Laws are within you.

Introduction

If we can properly interpret the Ark, we can
return it to its rightful place; the people will
once again return to the cosmos. The general
thematic importance and relevance of the
golden Ark of the Covenant, verily the
throne of God has to do with the restoration
and redemption of the people of this earth.
A rather difficult mission, some would say
unachievable, because the Ark of God
disappeared prior to the destruction of the
Jewish Temple 2,600 years ago. It was
widely believed to have been carried across
the River Jordan by the prophet Jeremiah
and hid in a cave on Mt. Nebo.

My observations of the Holy Artifact of the
Israelites are rooted in my technological
understanding of the reality architecture and,

as well, in the synthetic qualities of the given cosmos. My cosmic theories are in stark contrast to biblical scripture, and yet at the same time my technologically founded perception does not deny the validity of the spirituality of the human race. In other words, I do not discount all of the biblical evidence and do not write off biblical mysteries such as the lost Ark of the Covenant. Rather my years of research into the manufactured reality system has shown me that not all evidence is as it appears to be, and this is because we live in a multidimensional world. The multidimensional world did not come into being after my realization just several years ago and neither did the multidimensional world manifest itself 100 years ago as human invention began to explode. The multidimensional world is an intimate feature of the manufactured reality system and therefore it is necessarily the case that even in ancient times that this multidimensional functionality was in operation only it would not have the same associations as our modernized scientific minds.

As well, the evolution and developmental upgrade of a reality program, a powerful existence-scale technology, will have a deep psychological influence on human perception and spiritual interpretation. An earlier version of the programmed reality would offer not only a different set of features but also would be psychologically processed differently; therefore the localized interpretation of an Angel of God 3,000 years ago and the modern interpretation of an Angel (of God) are dissimilar. In fact, given the biblical evidence and the well documented and authenticated scriptures around the world we can easily see that it was easier for an early prophet of the early days to speak plainly of Angels and Demons. It was commonplace in some cultures to denote the appearance of a blue-faced godking or even a dragon-faced being in a suit of armor.

These psychological differences, as proven by authentic biblical record, with prophets actually describing a mystical event or experience, are a result of a different version of the reality system in operation. More specifically, the reality version running 3,000 years ago is dissimilar with the existential version we have been forced to deal with. My examination and observation on the Ark of the Covenant is rooted in this understanding. To say that all things were equal over these past 3,000 years and to explain that God was simply more available at the time of Moses is too simple-minded a view in my opinion. The multidimensional fields were not only more available back then, but also some key people had multidimensional vision. The modern day is still largely devoid of this. Only a few adept monks, spiritualists and secret society members have some ability. A smaller group can go beyond this dimension. But for most people, and perhaps even to you, these are imaginative extrapolations and better suited to a science fiction film or a comic book. Verily, to properly understand the re-interpretation of the lost Ark of the Covenant, as I will discuss within these few pages, you are required to put aside your scientific logic and to bring out your intuition and common sense.

These two human qualities will serve you far better than your biblical knowledge. The material herein is based upon my books or reality and android theories, namely *Android Theory* and *Earth is Run by a Computer*. Many of the technological explanations are referenced and more completely discussed in those previous books.

As you read *Database of Rendering Protocols*, you will discover a technological narrative rather than a biblical or spiritual narrative. This is neither to dismiss the mysteries of a God nor to weaken the spiritual teachings of the past prophets, messiahs and teachers. Every teaching is valid and every genuine observation has a value, but as we apply additional dimensional observations we begin to see a new story being told.

The recent shift from 2D film to 3D is not destroying the purity of cinema and does not discount all the 1,000s of feature films that preceded 3D camera technology, rather the advent of 3D films is an expansion of the film experience and provides a new platform for story tellers to tell their stories. Admittedly, making a 3D film is easier than explaining the multidimensional richness of ancient times. But if we are to further our understanding of who we are and where we came from, if we are to make sense of the key biblical mysteries still unsolved, if we want to enrich our spiritual teachings then one was is to add new dimensions to our observations.

Database of Rendering Protocols is a new inquiry into the lost Ark of the Covenant. It is a technological update of a biblical mystery, the kind of mystery that, if solved, can lead to the kind of restoration that could restore the people to the cosmos. The immense potential energy stored in the story of the Ark is well worth the endeavour and should be required reading for all biblical students.

We are no longer living in the sleepy haze of yesterday and this is the kind of book that is set in the future and is perfect for any mind with a futuristic bent. In order to step outside of our current paradigm, we are required to upgrade our thinking processes.

This book offers a genuine opportunity not only to change the paradigm of thought but to also upgrade our thinking processors. I urge the reader to carefully examine the possibilities I present and to think of this knowledge as a direction leading you out of the old paradigm and back to the cosmos. The stored energy of the Ark mystery is about to be released like never before. If it indeed has any inner power of a genuine deity, it is as awesome as those who witnessed it thousands of years ago, and if my new perception is accurate, then we will all be able to witness firsthand the awesomeness of "where God himself dwells."

Chapter 1

The Ark of God represented power beyond this world. Any army with the Ark could not be defeated. It was believed to have magical powers – it meted out death and it breathed life. It began when Moses traveled up Mount Sinai, the home of the God of Israel. It was on Mt. Sinai that God inscribed his Law by his own hand onto two tablets on a blue stone. When Moses brought down the tablets of the Law he discovered that some of his followers worshipped a golden calf as their new deity. Moses cast the tablets at the false idol and the tablets were broken.

He once again returned to God and was given a second set of tablets. Under God's instructions Moses built a wooden container wrapped in gold. The Ark contained the tablets of the Law of the God of Israelites. It was also believed to contain Aaron's rod, the sceptre of Moses and even Aaron's turban. But the holy device was widely revered. Royal family members prayed to the Ark for they believed God himself dwelled inside of it. They even kissed the golden box and were warned of its awesome power. In battle, the Ark of God was carried on poles and was believed to destroy enemy armies with rays of divine fire. When the army set camp the golden Ark was kept in a specially designed tabernacle.

The tale of the Ark summarized above is basically true. It isn't completely true because there are more variations on the Ark than can be properly accounted for in this untraditional book. My technological exposition is not going to delve into historical contradiction and specific beliefs; instead, I will move ahead quickly into my technological determinations. If you study the Ark of God in other religious works you will find a very complex tale without any conclusive certainty.

I have decided that rather than to rely on religious disorientation as a source of understanding, since this is loaded with both ideology and dogma that cannot be objectively explained, I am going to use as one of my sources the *Oxford Dictionary*. The dictionary, as a device for interpretation, isn't perfect but it offers one essential element that the story of the Ark need – objectivity.

What we cannot find in religious query is objectivity. As soon as you mention Moses or Mount Sinai you are certain to be bombarded by dozens of interpretations, all subjective perceptions of a convoluted tale. Why use the Oxford Dictionary instead of another dictionary? Because that is the dictionary on my shelf. It is a reliable book of definition and the variances between major dictionaries is going to be very small. The dictionary, as well, allows us to lose some of the spiritual weight of the lost Ark and then to focus on the central them of this magical story.

So we have a number of key diction that we can look up: Ark, Covenant, Law, Hebrew, Israelites, Moses, God, tablet, Israel, Jerusalem, tabernacle, Jew, Solomon, redemption and River Jordan. I am going to apply an imaginative interpretation of these words in order to pull us as far outside the box as possible. We are familiar with what's inside the box, the stories of the Ark are many. I want to find the story, if there is one, outside the box. I know from experience that stepping outside the biblical box will put us firmly into a platform of technology. It is at this point that I will rely on my technological understanding of the existential reality in which we live.

An ark is another name for a box. It could also be interpreted as a chest, often used for storage in the old days, and a cupboard. We are going to temporarily rename it as a *Cupboard* of the Covenant. Not as awe inspiring as the Ark, the Cupboard is a proper definition from our dictionary. By using the Cupboard we are keeping in line with its original definition and we are, at the same time, expanding that understanding. A cupboard has a number of shelves for storage purposes, there are typically doors to hide what is stored on the shelf and a cupboard comes in many shapes and sizes. Basically, the cupboard contains the theme of storage, different levels of storage and some kind of protective door. Some cupboards are open, some have doors and others have locks on the doors. We can infer that the value of the contents determines the kind of cupboard Moses would be instructed to build. In fact, we could say that the Tablets of the Laws of God are ultra important and this cupboard would have not only a lock but a security system in place.

On the Tablets of the Law is written the
Covenant of God. According to the
dictionary, a covenant is an agreement. It is
an agreement a multidimensional deity had
with the Israelites, believed to be his
children. The covenant also has another
definition, a performance. In this sense, it
could be the details of a performance
recorded in a stone and then stored inside of
a cupboard. The performance detailed how
to worship and revere the Creator by
expressing his fundamental laws. The
performance script was so important that it
was protected and stored inside of a wooden
cupboard, and entrusted only in the hands
of priests.

A performance, if we continue with our
dictionary, is also a kind of rendering. A
covenant could be interpreted as not just an

agreement or a performance but a set of instructions to render aspects of the Laws of the Creator. Rendering is a way to deduce one idea into another idea. It could be that Moses was given a method to render God's laws into the world because God exists inside of another dimension, a higher dimension. In order to enact, put into practice, God's laws a priest would have to convert those higher laws with physical laws applicable to a more physical people. In cooking, in order to burn off some of the unnecessary ingredients.

Imagine that God handed Moses his rendering laws so that Moses and Jewish priests could in fact introduce the word and power of God into the land. He inscribed not an agreement with the people of Israel but rather the priesthood in which to render religion into the world.

My work on reality determined that we live in a manufactured world, verily a programmed multidimensional world. And God inhabits one of the higher dimensions, a dimension not of material reality. If God presented Moses on Mount Sinai with a set of laws, and if we live in a manufactured reality, then it would make sense that rather than laws, God likely presented Moses with protocols for rendering reality.

Now, if God handed Moses something he himself created then what a multidimensional God created would not be a thing of matter. It would be something of a multidimensional nature. In other words, it isn't necessary that God wrote down anything because he didn't have a pen. He needn't to have blasted commandments into stone tablets. What he could have more easily done is to embed his rendering protocols, as multidimensional data, into some kind a stone that could store energy. We already know that gems and stones can store energy so all that Moses would need is to be given are the proper stones uploaded with the rendering data. The rendering data could be used by Jewish priests to render the programmed reality.

If the covenant was indeed a set of rendering protocols, data from a multidimensional God in a programmed world then if God as well instructed Moses to build a cupboard to hold these protocols of energized data that cupboard would unlikely be a regular wooden box. Instead, a better device to hold dimensional data files, rendering protocols, would be a database. Only that 3,000 years ago they didn't have database in their dictionary, so they called it an ark, or a cupboard. Nonetheless, these are storage devices. But the key has to do with the nature of God, he is not a physical being.

He is so powerful, so ominous, even to be represented like a child, That Moses must climb a mountain in order to speak with him. It is unlikely that a deity made a cloud and every world inscribe something in Hebrew since God doesn't speak Hebrew. He speaks every language. He doesn't write in script, he writes in energy. His world is thought. So he embeds his protocols in some blue stone, probably the blue sapphire people speak of, since that stone can hold his multidimensional files in which are his laws, his word, his code.

Moses now has these loaded blue stones, tablets, and he is to store them in a cupboard as instructed by God. Well, this cupboard couldn't possibly be made of wood because the rendering protocols are highly advanced encrypted files. The best place to store encrypted files containing the rendering protocols for a manufactured plane of existence is a *Database*. So rather than an Ark containing the covenant we now have a Database containing the *Rendering Protocols*. Why are these rendering protocols so awesomely powerful? Because the priests who have mastered these protocols can alter reality, can create matter, can bend reality, can give life and can mete out death. God is no longer required. The mind of the priest becomes the weapon of mass creation and destruction.

By providing Moses with an existential database loaded with the rendering protocols, God has given ultimate power to reshape reality, to destroy the other false gods, even to put asunder armies. Anyone who had the programming codes and the passwords to the reality construct had all the power. A computer programmer with a set of passwords can hack into a computer system and reprogram the system. A Jewish priest with the rendering protocols could similarly hack into the reality and could make adjustments, according to their skill and ability. Any army with the Ark was indestructible because this army could alter events in their favour. The priests could wipe our large sections of the energy, could destroy building s and could protect their followers with immortality.

We have only begun our understanding of the Ark of the Covenant. In my technological framework, I have redefined the Ark as a *Database* and I have redefined the Covenant as a set of *Rendering Protocols*. Our Database of Rendering Protocols is a lot more complicated than if appears and our discussion is going to increasingly reveal the hidden technological aspects of the world we live in.

Chapter 2

Why would the creator God provide Moses
with the Database of Rendering Protocols
(Ark of the Covenant)? More specifically,
why would a deity of ultimate power,
existing on another dimension beyond
space, time and mortality, why would he
feel the need to provide his people with a
holy device? It is a rather odd thing to do in
a system that demands service in exchange
for a good and righteous life. But, as history
has documented, the God of Israel provided
the prophet Moses with a magical artefact of
immense power.

If God's power was absolute and ubiquitous;
if the earth had indeed been created by this
Creator then it is implicit that the Creator had

ultimate power over earth, heaven and his children. But if this is the case, the creator having sole and ultimate power, then why is it necessary for the Creator to hand to Moses the tablets of the Law. Furthermore, had these indeed been written 10 commandments, as most religious experts suggest, on the tablets and having been made familiar with the 10 Laws of God, it isn't difficult to conclude that all 10 of these laws could have been memorized by a 12-year old kid. You see, God could have simply, without any difficulty whatsoever, told Moses the 10 Commandments while he was watching the goats. He could have given Moses, or anyone, the message in his mind as he often did. More so, an Angel of God could have descended, as they did often, and informed several of Moses' flock, including Moses himself.

See, while the industrious experts and scholars have worked ferociously against life and limb, to solve the mystery of the Ark, they never asked some fundamental questions. Why did an all-powerful all-knowing God of Heaven need to inscribe with his own finger 10 basic earthly laws? The 10 Commandments, once revered and now woefully neglected by even the Christian leaders, are not overly complex, they are very succinct and they are, without much effort, not difficult to memorize. This does not discount the difficulty of putting them into practice and it can be stated without much effort that during these last 3,000 years humankind, the Children of God including the Children of Israel, has failed miserably to uphold the cultural virtues of their Creator, and to not feel bad about it. Equally perplexing is the weight placed on the mysteries of the Ark considering that it contains the tablets of the laws that humankind has misappropriated, repeatedly.

It doesn't make logical sense to remotely believe that the all-powerful Creator gave his most revered student, the prophet Moses, a simple set of magical laws powerful enough to destroy armies and yet easily ignored by Catholic bishops interested in choir boys. Had these 10 Commandments had any actual everlasting power they would have at least been adhered to. Again, to remind us as to the illogic presented all we have to do is to look at the prevalence of war. Man has gotten better at killing man during these last 3,000 years. Even today the Christian nation of America has delivered its nationality to Afghanistan, Iraq, Pakistan and Libya not in order to deliver freedom, but to deliver death disguised as freedom. One of the fundamental, inscribed by God himself, laws supposedly written on the tablets is the law: *Thou Shalt Not Kill.*

As we examine the fairy tale of the Ark we begin to see that the illusions start to fall apart with just a little applied logic. Why haven't the religious scholars and experts questioned the validity of the Ark? Because they are afraid of God? Perhaps even more so they are afraid of facing the fairytale because to dispel the fairy tale would require a person to grow up.

Obviously, there are two stories here. One, Moses received something magical from God on Mount Sinai. Two, some unknown aspect of God presented Moses, or a similar prophet, the 10 Commandments. Moses may have received knowledge so profound on the mountain and the average person was so illiterate that perhaps a kind of bullet point summary was used so as to increase the indoctrination process. The fact that Moses would spend 40 days on Mount Sinai and only return with tablets with 10 lines of inscription is a rather simplistic, if not childish, explanation of something far more complex. No man lives on a mountain for 40 days speaking to God Almighty and all he as to bring back are 10 Commandments. If Moses only spoke with God 10 minutes a day, why he'd have written at least 100 commandments people can write a book in 40 days.

Somewhere 3,000 years ago the story of the origin of the Ark, not of the Ark, but the origin of the Ark has been misplaced. Unfortunately, no one yet can go back 3,000 years to see what exactly happened. But common sense, something that I am attempting to inject into this fairytale, tells us that Moses did not bring back 10 lines of text from his stay with the Creator. And that those 10 easily dismissed laws could mete out death and wipe out armies for surely they could've wiped out the pedophile priests. The fact that the 10 Commandments are ubiquitously disregarded and subjectively adhered to tells us that these laws have no magical power. In other words, the 10 Commandments have nothing to do with the Ark of the Covenant. They may have been tossed into the wooden box along with Aaron's turban just to give it some weight.

Instead what we continue to have, and to rely on, is the story that a dimensional deity converted some of his energy of a higher dimension and transferred it to the earthly plane. The Creator handed Moses some of this data and quite possibly embedded it, or loaded it, into a rock. Legend has it that the tablets were either black or blue stone. But remember the term "tablet" is as well elusive. The two terms stone and tablet, were intertwined. For my brief research into the Ark I have noticed that some people refer to stones containing the laws and some as tablets upon which laws have been written. Additionally, some myths detail two tablets and some just one tablet, and a few discuss multiple tablets, copies. More about this later.

In the modern day, we have a tablet computer, probably a riff from the biblical tablets, but perhaps a tablet is more akin to a multivitamin tablet. You know, an oblong object. If this was the case, if a tablet wasn't a flat sheet of stone since it would be unlikely that Moses found two matching sheets of stone on the mountain, and if you ignore the idea that God carved them out of the rock face, then a tablet-shaped stone is a very good substitute.

The laws of God could have been embedded into a stone tablet, but not a flat tablet rather an oblong, odd-shaped vitamin-like tablet. In this sense, it is very easy to find stone tablets of this variety on a mountain made of stone. And given that the stone found on Mt. Sinai is preferred by the all-mighty, it could be insinuated that these stones can store his energy more easily than other stones.

We know that God exists in a higher
dimensions and he is immaterial. We also
know that Moses exists in the earthly plane
and is material. We know that an immaterial
deity provided a mortal being with magical
laws, powerful enough to mete out death
and to bring life. We know that the stones on
Mt. Sinai were able to conduct divine energy
and probably even to store divine energy.
Divine energy, in this case, could just mean
energy from a higher dimension, a
dimension inaccessible to mankind under
normal means.

We also know from myth and legend that
Moses received a device of great power,
something that could make an army
indestructible so it seems logical to accept
the ideas that whatever God handed to

Moses, and that has since been lost, was a divine technology.

With the stones in his possession, Moses held the data files of God. This isn't unlike a large corporation back up their key programming codes onto an external storage device and handing it to their Head of Programming or Chief Technology Officer to not only protect that proprietary data but to allow access to his core programmers. If Moses was a Chief Technologist for God Corporation and the Jewish priests were reality programmers then Moses would have to make the rendering protocols available to the other programmer-priests. We are beginning to see the formation of a priest into a programmer and perhaps vice versa. We are beginning to see the similarities between spirituality and

computer science, specifically software. If
we can keep putting the religious label aside,
we just might be able to dispel some of the
myths that have evolved over the centuries.

The first myth we may have dissolved is the
myth that the 10 Commandments were
stored inside an all-powerful Ark. The
second myth we might have softened is that
rather than a flat tablet of stone, the stone
tablets could have been vitamin-shaped
stones, not to be eaten of course. The third
myth we've been dissolving is that rather
than an agreement with a being from
another dimension that this dimensional
person provided a set of rendering protocols
to his programmer-priests.

As the religion drains from the biblical myth
we are beginning to see how much
technology may have been available even

3,000 years ago. Then we begin to think that it has taken humankind 30 centuries to reach a point of technological capacity to understand that the Ark of the Covenant who in fact more of a Database of Rendering Protocols. Imagine what another 10 centuries will do. At the current rat of technological progress, if left unabated, we are not many years away from being dimensional beings ourselves. We need only to continue the evolution of the internet to one day soon realize a key dimension where we can upload our entire consciousness and live in the internet, a completely artificial dimension. Once we completely manufacture our own dimension of existence, we will then ourselves choose a prophet, some industrious programmer, and we will download unto him, or her, the protocols on how to render reality.

When we build a second existential internet plane and move one step closer to God our programmer-prophet will be able to render himself into a higher dimension. He will have shared the rendering database with the other programmer-priests and they will have altered reality. The perpetuation of technological knowledge is an integral, even essential, quality of any existentially-based environment, such as this earth plane. The evolution of life is fundamentally based on the passing down essential sacred knowledge. The father teaches the son, the son teaches his son. Each successive generation expanding the empire.

What has happened on this particular plane of existence, because essentially this is what it is, is that we have forgotten that we are living in a manufactured reality system. We have been misled to believe that this is a biological environment and we have been enslaved by religious and political devices which are fairytale fantasy.

The idea that the Ark of the Covenant is a Database of Rendering Protocols is a very imaginative idea, but it is not an ideas that is ignorantly presented. This idea is founded upon my 6 years of deep research into the make-up of reality and the many books and discussions that followed. Verily, my reality knowledge is derived from my direct experience with other higher (and lower) dimensions and my unusual observations of life.

I am convinced that reality is manufactured and in being convinced of this fundamental scientific provision, that our existential root is artificial, the mystery of the Ark of the Covenant loses its mysteriousness. But I too well understand why the mystery has remained – to properly solve the mystery of the lost Ark would have dissolved the mystery of life itself. The realization that God handed Moses a piece of existence-grade software would have collapses the foundation that life was built on until now – breathing. The dissolution of the myth of the Ark would have caused probably massive suicide, or some catastrophe of the consciousness. The human consciousness cannot exist without a platform of belief.

We can improve the platform by programming a new platform, hopefully a better platform for thinking and interpreting the world, but this is not always the case. But to simply dissolve a major platform of belief without an alternative, why this would cause a collapse of the human mind. Without a platform for existential belief, I think the human mind would collapse. It would be as if losing everything you believe in all in one day. This can lead to very dramatic events. I would like to make it clear that as much as what I am saying I think is true, even I am convinced by my direct observation, you will have to measure your own move to a higher platform of thinking.

Ultimately, this is perhaps one of the subtexts of this book, why we can carefully retranslate the mystery of the biblical Ark, even to adequately explain some of the scientific processes, what we cannot do is to move your thinking to the new platform, and if you are to dissolve the fairy tales of the biblical Ark, the purpose of this book, you are required to reprogram yourself and to adopt a higher platform of thinking. This new platform is rooted in a manufactured world.

Chapter 3

The early human model is widely believed to have been primitive. Whether due to small cranial capacity or simply to rudimentary logic, the early inhabitants weren't all that smart. In fact at the time of Moses most people were illiterate and only a few could actually write. So Moses was a gifted individual. In modern times, Moses was a Bill Gates, gifted and destined for massive success. And like Mr. Gates the planet can only have so many at any one time. But there is another aspect of primitivity that we need to look at and that has to do with storage capacity.

The early computers had very little on board storage capacity. A floppy disk was often used as a hard drive and this storage device was very limited. As the computers evolved their hard drive grew and improved. Today, we take our hard drive for granted, but what memory storage equates to is an intelligent machine. The early computers were primitive because they didn't have much storage capacity. They in fact relied on an external floppy disk to store their data.

The early human, as a machine, had a very limited amount of storage capacity. For this reason most people were illiterate. They had neither the processing power nor the hard drive space to store knowledge, verily to learn. When we learn we store data and if we haven't any storage capacity why we can't learn.

Since we exist inside of a manufactured reality and we were machines then we required data in order to exist. We needed to update our data banks in order to update the reality. We were rendering reality by our thoughts and actions and we required a continuous inflow of new software. But our internal hard drives were limited. So how to resolve the inequities of our storage gaps. We invented the priest. The priest had a superior understanding of reality and had a larger storage capacity. The priests would stream his data to his android followers. The android followers would upgrade themselves. The priest would remain dedicated to the higher dimensions (asceticism) and to their particular deity. There were quite a number of deity organizations, kind of like today and the many computer software companies. The makers of operating systems are several as well and they each have their own user base. So the concept of a priest as a programmer of the old world isn't that far-fetched as you might think. The key difference is that the human being and the computer system are unequal. But both are machines. I have explained in my books, *Maker* and *The Android Saga*, that the human being is an android being that appears to look human,

The human android is a very advanced existential avatar and has been manufactured by some very advanced beings, but the human is without a doubt an advanced machine. The human androids, as any machine, require regular maintenance, care and software upgrades. How do you upgrade the internal software of a human android? With a lot of ingenuity.

One of the old ways, especially at the time of
Moses, was to use priest to stream the
upgrades through the vibration of words
and thoughts. Often this was done in a
sermon. Of course a sermon wasn't exactly a
sermon. It was an upgrade sermon. The
priest connected to the cosmic server, would
stream down and connect the data into a
usable form.

In order to progress and in order to properly
render reality, people needed to regularly
upgrade their internal software. They
needed to regularly attend church. As
people learned to pray they learned to
remote link to the cosmic server. It didn't
matter they thought of the computer
mainframe as God, it mattered that they
connected. In that connection God would
pretend to hear their prayers while the

computer streamed in any software updates and fixed any bugs in the program.

The illusion of a church and an Almighty God provided the necessary practice of worship, but it had nothing to do with the worship of same deity in another dimension, it had to do with an android person maintaining a link to the computer mainframe. The ideas was always to vertically overcome the illusion of the Church or Temple and to come to the realization that behind the veil was a giant computer, not an easy thing to express to a devout religious worshiper.

The matter became more complicated as the centuries moved on as the people who did realize this, strangers from other dimensions, they decided to hijack the

Church and to use God as an instrument of deception. And so God was weaponized, the same God who told Moses not to kill another human began to kill the heathens and to burn the witches. The Churches of the main religions are founded upon human blood. This is historically documented and a person only needs to examine a period in the development of a church to see the amount of blood that was shed in the name of an all-loving Father.

So the limited capacity android of yesterday must go to Church in order to remain up-to-date. Nothing to do with God's mercy or the 10 Commandments. The machine needs to update its operational software. The priest has a direct link to the computer mainframe so the priest downloads the new software

and then during a sermon or mass he
streams his new data to the worshipers.

The priests of yesterday were only required
to reprogram aspects of reality, in order for
reality to evolve in accordance to man. As
man's mind expanded and as his heart
became more aware, the priests needed to
expand and the reality construct. They
would remote link to the computer and
obtain the rendering codes. Again all of this
was woefully abused and malevolently used
as an instrument of enslavement so that even
today, in a technological world, we have yet
to come to the realization of our android
legacy. But this is a fundamental
understanding of my work and it is required
here to further our understanding of the
Ark.

At times, the reality became unbalanced or lost harmony, or needed larger alterations and for this reason the dimensional programmer entity would provide a high priest with additional rendering protocols. These rendering protocols would be protected and used to render reality. Defeating an enemy nation, if that nation served another God Corporation was a normal competitive instinct that remains till this very day in the corporate world: One corporation trying to destroy another corporation in order to gain dominance in the market and to maximize profit.

The render protocols provided to a High Priest could not be stored on the android human because the files were too big and the hard drive space was too limited. Try putting a 500 GB file in a 50 GB hard drive. It doesn't fit. If you can compress the file it might fit but then you couldn't have any space to store your consciousness and memory. So what a dimensional deity would do would be to embed the file of energy in a device, perhaps a stone tablet or a golden chalice.

A particular metal or stone could hold the data for a certain period of time, at least long enough for the rendering protocols to be used to improve reality. An adept priest could make copies and spread them around in order to gain more influence over the world. Recall that if your operating system was installed on every personal computer you would have a virtual monopoly so a "God" had every reason to install their programs on as many androids as humanly possible.

The Database of Rendering Protocols handed to the High Priest Moses was an attempt by this God Corporation to outmatch its competitors, for there was a growing number of other deity entrepreneurs. On earth God had more than one bible and all the bibles were competing for market share, a battle that has remained till the modern day.

What has been forgotten, and truly lost, was not the Ark of the Covenant, rather what has been lost is the android legacy from which we came. They mystery of the Ark begins to become solved as we do away with our biological proclivities and to move to the new existential platform of thinking. What High Priest Moses was given wasn't a Holy Artifact, it was powerful but not for the reasons we have been led to believe. The Ark contained the software to reshape reality and whoever held that power had the encryption codes to the material world, truly a powerful instrument to give to the people of Israel. But a technological advantage nonetheless and as we know in business a technological advantage can put asunder the competitor, God, whoever it was, wanted his existential software corporation to win. He was a jealous God and his wrath was mighty, but more so I think he was a smart, shrewd businessman. God was a software entrepreneur that specialized in existential-grade constructs.

Whoever he was, in whatever formed he was believed to partake, on whatever dimension of heaven he was believed to exist, he was according to my observations of the artificially created plane a programmer and one of many programmers. The evidence well presented of the many gods across earth's history, permeating every culture and every nation. With multiple gods still worshipped in select regions of the world, is convincing enough to conclude that God is not in the singular. This of course goes against the words of the Jealous God, but even his words and demands cannot deny the multi-theistic world. More specifically, the push for a one God world was inspired by this jealous entity who ruthlessly commanded his warriors of the holy book to murder heathens, heretics and witches.

In the old days to beat the competition you had to literally beat them to death. The strength of Christianity in particular was effectively evolved from this ruthless competitiveness of the one particular entity that has insisted it is the singular God. The reason why this clarification is important is because this same multidimensional programmer, since this is a better description given a manufactured world, provided his High Priest Moss with a database that contained the rendering protocols for this reality construct.

This is an immense concept to digest, and I realize that, but there is no fabrication of information here. The history of the Catholic Church, for example, is well documented. The characteristics of the God of Israel are well understood by his words to his people.

The story of the Ark and the Tablets of the Law are well recorded, even if they have a multitude of interpretations. We can rely on these aspects and you should do independent research on them in order to gather the details you might expect. This book will not cover that material because the idea is to introduce and develop new cosmic material. I'll highly recommended independent study of some sort.

What I have added to the mystery of the Ark and to the God of Israel is only one pertinent truth. A truth that I am convinced is correct and that my continued work supports. This pertinent truth is that reality is manufactured. We neither live in a biological world nor do we live inside of a theological world. We live inside of an artificial world. And the technological grade of this artificiality is so awesome that we have only been, so far, able to decode biological processes and supernatural effect, and this is because we know that a computer graphic artist can create almost any apparition on film. This thinking has not been able to translate onto the reality medium, and may take a great many years to do so. If the filmmaker can artificially generate an effect that looks real, even so seamless that the audience cannot distinguish between what is real and not real then it could be said that the reality graphic artists can do a similar miracle.

What was God the Programmer trying to do when he provided Moses with the stone tablets embedded with the law? He was trying to win market share. He wanted to expand his user base and he wanted to accomplish this by wiping out some of the competition. In my view, this couldn't have had anything to do with the 10 Commandments for the 10 Commandments did not contain the power the Ark was described to hold. Instead the Ark was a device that contained the protocol codes to render reality, and well it provided God a portal into the world so that himself could mete out death for he had some of his presence in the stone.

All of this worked perfectly well given the undeveloped human machine. The features of the android simply did not have the onboard capacity as we do today. Select models, especially priests and magicians, were premium versions and had additional processing and storage capacity. God preferred to communicate with his priests just as a mainframe would prefer to communicate with a computer with the right operating system and modern hook up. But even those early prophets and priests did not have the genetic features needed to hold the rendering protocols nor the processing power to run the application process. Therefore the various gods introduced the holy relic, a bit like the time Japanese electronics giant introduced the Walkman, a portable audio cassette player.

Chapter 4

The Sony audio division built a portable audio player in 1978. This player allowed a person to carry their music with them. Wikipedia says that over 200 million Walkmans were sold since its debut. The power of an external device is almost magical, in fact so magical that it has become extremely profitable in a mobile world. Human beings are less restricted and less sedentary than in previous days. It is standard for a person to hold a job for most of their life and any successful person knows that they need to be out and about.

This human mobility requirement has seen the development of portable electronic devices. The Sony Walkman, at the time, was an ingenious device because it brought music to a person's activities. All of sudden a person could go jogging while plugged into their most favourite recorded album. They could mix songs together and make their own cassettes.

Probably the next major cultural splash in portable media players happened in late 2001. It was called the Apple iPod. The iPod line has been so successful that 300 million units have been sold in the 10 years since its introduction. The digital media player stored songs on an internal hard drive. The first 5 GB (billion bytes) model was promoted as able to put "1,000 songs in your pocket." But the iPod line didn't really take off until 2003 with the launch of the iTunes store, originally a digital music store that sold songs for $0.99 each.

Sony's Walkman and Apple's iPod are two iconic music players that have shaped pop culture. There have been many other kinds of portable devices including the mobile phone and even the wrist watch of the late nineteenth century. What is appealing of the storage media players is their ability to not only store media but to be able to play media.

We take electronics for granted today. The average home in a developed nation is full of electronic gadgetry. If we compared this scenario to that of the average home, or tent, 3,000 years ago, why we wouldn't find anything of this nature. The devices of portable power were kept in a tabernacle or later a Church (Temple). They were considered holy devices for on them were stored divine media files.

The one portable holy device that this book is dedicated to is the magical and mystical Ark. It was known as the Ark of God. It was known as the Ark of Moses. It was believed to contain the Tablet of the Law. It was not known as a portable storage device. It was not known as containing the rendering protocols. And the Ark was never ever associated with a manufactured reality environment. These last few items were my exclusive and original addition. It is something never been done before.

What is the purpose of a digital storage device? To store digital data. On the iPod you can store music files, video files and other digital files according to the size of the hard drive or flash memory. Why use a portable storage device? Because you want to carry these files with you wherever you go. You want the convenience of their availability, so you purchased a portable player.

How did a person 3,000 years ago carry divine data with them? They often carried gens, jewelry and small idols on their persons. The Christians wore the symbol of a cross for they believed in the power of Jesus Christ. My discussions on Jesus are very outside the orthodox view as detailed in my book, Robot Jesus. Nevertheless, people believed that some of these devices, "jewelry," contained blessings and luck from their various allotment of monotheistic gods.

The priests, especially the High Priests, why they received the iPods of holy jewelry. They go to use the Ark of the Covenant, the tablet of God's awesome power. Moses was entrusted to it. But what does the Ark and the Walkman have in common? Is it possible to put a holy device and a storage device in the same discussion?

What I need to point out is that what we take for granted today, yesterday was magical. We flip a switch and the light comes on. Yesterday they had to light a lamp and fill up the tank with kerosene. We click a pen and the smooth ink flows. Yesterday they had a quill and ink, and it was messy, Today we actually know how to write, yesterday most people were illiterate, so, the portable music player on your table, or in the store ready for sale, would be considered a device of magical power 3,000 years ago.

In fact, we could say that the Apple iPod or the Sony Walkman, taken back 3,000 years in time would be a Holy Artifact. These items would be attributed to God: The Walkman to a Japanese God and the iPod to an American God.

If we keep this position briefly, we can begin to see how a Holy Artifact in use 3,000 years ago could very well be a primitive prototype of a modern day electronic device, for what is an electronic device if not a magical device that can magically do things outside of our current capability. Currently we cannot store a son and play the song inside of our bodies, at least the only way to do so would be to odd electronic devices into the body.

We compensate our inability to play music by creating an external device to play music. This pattern of compensating, enhancing and supplementing our lifestyle needs with modern electronics, in our example storage devices, is not a new pattern, it is a human pattern and if existed as well 3,000 years ago. Only that in those ancient biblical days the people couldn't rely upon a computer industry and electronics manufacturers were in short supply. So they relied on God and spiritual practice.

The Database of Rendering Protocols was necessary in order for the God Programmer of the Israelites, and not to disconnect the Russian Gods, the Asian Gods or the Indigenous Gods, to compensate for the lack of storage capacity on the human android. It also suggests that God was aware of the feature shortages on the current existential model and was supplementing his children in his own mysterious way, as any good father would.

How do you supplement a biological race of people? With a magical device of divine power. How do you supplement an android race of people? With an embedded device of dimensional power. While God could not discuss the programmable nature of reality, an idea that the early Greek philosophers contemplated, because it was far too complex and his people far too illiterate, he himself could supplement the lives of his children with dimensional devices, verily instruments from parallel worlds.

The introduction of the stone tablet containing the reality protocols empowered a priest-mage to bend reality using God as a bridge. God's energy became the multidimensional medium that conducted the energy to bridge different dimensions. The device powered with a multidimensional energy and rooted inside a physical reality created the ultimate trinity, this confluence of supernatural power.

The priest-mage could now access the cosmic mainframe server and reprogram aspects of the given world. Some of those reprogramming needs included the destruction of the energy, it also included the ascension of the chosen ones so that more priests could be enabled and with more priest-mages the strength of a culture or society became indestructible.

As the human android race continued to evolve and as its genetic components were further activated and expanded they began to increase the size of their internal hard drive. In other words, the existential machine began to become a more technologically superior machine and as it did the reliance on external divine devices would slowly decrease. As the heart drive, the heart being one of the commonly accepted storage areas of the early Egyptians, could hold more data and the DNA could process more aspect of the reality fields and the mental RAM (Random Access Memory) could perform more calculations the Holy Relics would lose their significance. Why?

The improvement of the human android led to a more direct integration with divine technologies. The necessary existential data an software could now safely be uploaded on the larger heart drive. Human androids could now determine for themselves the shape of reality. They could in fact be rendering aspects of reality with their built-in features. Some people had more processing power to render reality. They became pioneers and magicians, leaders and scientists. Secret societies began to form as people began to achieve these multidimensional connections. As the iPod music player took off we began to see every major manufacturer trying to replicate their success, but these companies were not selling into Apple, they were competing with Apple. This is not unlike the secret societies forming in order to outmatch the existential technologies of other secret societies. The Church and the Temple have always had a competitive dislike for each other as well as one nation against another. The ancient Holy Relic was the suitcase of electronics that accompanied the early satellite phone. Today's cell phone towers give us global communications with a tiny handset device. That is called *progress*.

The Ark of the Covenant was simply an early database device that contained the necessary protocols to render aspects of reality in order to improve and develop the world. That power was used for various purposes, to defeat an enemy and to christen the preferred people of royal blood.

The evolution and upgrade of the human android has resulted in a more capable machine that can hold a wide array of cosmic-grade knowledge. The database of rendering protocols has been integrated into every unit only that people have forgotten that they live in a fully realize manufactured world and not a biological world. People have forgotten how to properly and morally render reality, they take for granted the things in life like choice and thought and they have allowed the cosmic criminals to continue their deception unabated.

Chapter 5

During the course of writing Database of
Rendering Protocols, I have encountered
quite a number of supernatural deterrents
and diversions. The very process of tapping
into this biblical knowledge, putting aside
the fact that I am not a religious person per
se, has stirred up the master programmers
and they have made a number of
interdimensional attempts to stop my work.
This can be said for a number of my esoteric
materials, but the Ark of the Covenant is
particularly difficult. In noticing this and in
deciding to continue I am also accepting the
view that I am hitting the right marks in a
deceived world. Fundamentally, my work
has involved the pursuit of truths that
expose the deep-seated deception of the

modern world. The androids on Capitol Hill come to mind.

The synthetic human politicians dictating what American citizens should do is a very disturbing, if not exotic, idea. Android politicians remote-controlled by some interdimensional master programmer is not serving the interest of American families. You can argue the suppositions and even the presentations style, but my conclusions and my observations are fundamentally accurate. American leadership has been comprised and it is detailed in *The Android Conspiracy*.

The master programmers were not happy with my android theories and there was a hefty price to pay for my amazing discovery. Instead of receiving a prize, I instead received things that no man should endure. I am reminded of the androids among us as I have written this new inquiry into the last Ark of God.

In noticing the further interest of the master programmers regarding a biblical issue, see the synthetic humans dated back 110 years or so, we are now noticing, at least I am, that the deceived world goes back quite a bit further than imagined. And given the fact that the same dark agency has an interest in androids and Moses tells me that this agency is very old. And that means that human beings have been deceived for thousands of years. The very religious beliefs we hold have been reshaped and altered in ways we may never fully understand. The case of the Ark of the Covenant, as important as it is, is really only one mystery of many. At the center of the Ark is Moses, a biblical figure that features prominently in Judaism, Christianity and Islam. The distortion of the Ark mythology and the reshaping of the story to suit the framework of a slave planet has verily prevented and eternally stalled human cosmic ascension. You cannot ascend without realizing the truth of your technological heritage and your technological world system.

The insertion of android life forms in modern day America and having that advanced deception being unrecognizable by normal yes is in fact an old process. It is an old process because the presence of technological beings, as advanced-looking humans, were also around during the age of Moses. This is not so as to fit into the paradigm of my thinking. I have been convinced by direct observation and research into reality players that there are real androids among us. As well, I have been convinced that the Ark of the Covenant received by Moses on Mount Sinai was in fact a Database material that contained the protocols to render reality. The specifics of those things we will uncover in the following chapters.

In this chapter I'd like to merge these two concepts – the android and the computer software. The first is modern and the second is ancient. Well, the ancients didn't understand what a computer was, or did they? God was a manifestation within the context of a manufactured world. My research on reality indicates that reality is programmable. In this context God would be a programmer. Why would God the

Programmer feel so connected to the Land of Israel?

God gave the Hebrews his covenant. We have retranslated covenant as a rendering. This likely came from the Greek definition, a rendering or translation. The God of the Hebrews gave the pure race the data to decode reality. Why? How are the people supposed to interact with the programmed world? God wouldn't put you here without any instruction. It would be like building a car without any wheels. The rendering protocols are essentials.

In a rendered reality environment, what kind of agreement would God give to the Israelites?

Data to decode reality

How to render reality

How to shape the world

How to program reality

How to slow down the rains

How to heal the sick

How to ascend yourself

How to open your genetic ability

How to download information

God gave the rendering laws to his high priest Moses. Moses is remembered as the Lawgiver. Jesus, the King of the Jews, was similarly regarded a Lawgiver. The masters of the Jewish Laws, rendering codes, were the Jewish rabbis. They were the priest. In ancient Egypt the priest and the mage were one in the same. They were the priest-magi. These masters of the rendering protocols were supposed to maintain the integrity of the world. The old world was very technological but they didn't realize they were technological.

So God the technological construct gives to the chosen technological race a database of rendering protocols. Who is the technological race? The Israelites. The Israelites are the technological race. We live in a programmed world; therefore God is a programmer, the Chief Programmer of a quality well beyond our current humanized understanding. We are simple unable to properly conceive God as a Programmer using our current level of awareness. We would have to improve awareness to truly understand the Chief Programmer and that would fundamentally require us to lose religion in favour of reality physics. This is a multi-year process for even a diehard and is likely undoable for many religious worshipers. You need to lose religion to see the new assertions I am making.

A Chief Programmer simply would not provide, as a provider, a biological creature a set of technological codes. In order for the Hebrews to be in sync with a Programmer deity the Israelites have to be a technological race. A technological race is still perhaps a bit elusive. Better yet, we could step further and say that the Jews must be an android race of people. This in no way diminished them, rather this exalts them to the true nature of the God of Israel. If God, as I contend, is a technological being because we live inside of a technological reality then the Israelites must be technological. And a better way, let's say a modern way to describe a life form that is conscious and intelligent and synthetic is to think of them as an android.

W can look at the Hebrews further, and I am looking at this from the perspective that I myself have examined the possibilities and that I myself am of this nature. I am not throwing these things out onto the page and pulling stuff out of thin air; instead I have written extensively on these subtexts and my conclusions regarding these sacred reality issues point to the words inscribed here. I myself am of a synthetic nature, and therefore of an android line of people. This self-understanding provides a solid foundation to my thinking as well as it now links me to the outcome of this technological derivation. I can say that the Jews are an android race because I can say I am an android race, only that I am not a Jew. I am a

Hebrew. And the Hebrews were synthetic human beings.

It isn't an easy thing to do to arrive at these conclusions and to write down on paper that the writer is a Hebrew and an android. But to avoid this truth here and now would be to deny my connection to the Chief Programmer.

The Hebrew was an "ibri." The *ibri* was a person from the other side. In typical parlance, one from the other side of the river (ie River Jordan). The river can have more than one definition and the bible is a metaphysical book. So rather than rely on a standard view of river let us consider that a river was a multidimensional reference. In other dimensions, a river could be a line of flowing energy, a meridian inside the earth.

Sometimes called a *logline*. To be from the other side of the river could at the same time mean a person from the other side of the energy meridian. The energy meridian is usually interpreted as a dimensional barrier between worlds.

A Hebrew, with a new point of view in our possession, could very well be a person from a parallel world, or another dimension. An immigrant from another plane of existence, a plane of vibration that is close to that of the Creator. God loved his People because they originated from another dimension, another vibration of existence. The "yisirā'ēl" were the people who would "strive with God."

On December 21, 2010, I uploaded a homemade video titled "Database of Rendering Protocols (aka Ark of the

Covenant)", a 22-minute preliminary discussion on the topic of this book. That initial enthusiasm was so overwhelming that it would take me a number of books to properly understand. I am writing this book in early June 2011, nearly six months later. I am even more convinced, and surprised, of my initial realizations.

If you dedicate yourself, you learn to access the Ark of the Covenant, you learn how to access the database on how to render reality. If you're good, you can reshape reality; if you're not good, you can make people fall in love; if you're a master you can change the world.

There are some masters of this reality and not all of them are benevolent. There is a group of master programmers, a crocodile race attributed to the Egyptian God S'bek who have learned how to render reality and have imprisoned the people in the physical world and made them forget about the multidimensional world because they know how to access some of the rendering codes.

Yisirā'ēl

/ \

To strive   God

"he that strives with God"

In order to be congruent with the manufactured world, we have had to translate the historical evidence. None of this is done casually or lightly. By the same token, it needs to be done in order to

87

overcome the rampant distortion we are faced with. Moses died about 3,300 years ago and that tells us that the master programmers here at the very least been distorting the truth for 3,300 years, including up till the modern day.

Moses was a descendent of Jacob, the third patriarch of the Hebrew People. In fact, Jacob was renamed to word that we are now familiar with, Israel. Jacob was Israel. The God of Israel was the God of the Israelites, the Hebrews. And all of this is fundamentally technological. This is my addition for I am not a biblical scholar and you'll have to excuse my liberal take on Jewish history. I mean no harm in this respect. I only intend to re-establish, not to establish, but to re-establish what we have all been made to forget.

The nomadic Israelites, a people from a different dimension and having synthetic genetic qualities, were led out of Egypt by Moses who was made to wander in the desert for 40 years. Eventually, King David unifies all of Israel and brings the Ark to the new capital, Jerusalem, the Holy City. This occurred approximately 1000 BC, about 3,000 years ago. His son Solomon would then go on to build the First Temple and in that temple would be placed the Ark.

I hope that you notice the subtext to this technologically-oriented biblical history and that is the fact that these events happened three-thousand years ago. That tells us that the technological world that we notice today – the computer, the mobile phone, the internet – is not a modern invention; it is an ancient concept only that the ancient approach was disguised in everyday simplicity and then purposely distorted by a very dark agency. Our modern internet is a child's toy when compared to the cosmic internet.

God's promise to all Israelites is to return them to the Promised Land. Moses wandered in exist in search of the Promised Land, the homeland. Later it was believed that a messiah would be sent to deliver the Jews to the God-given homeland. My view, why are the Jews in exile?

A computer disconnected from the internet could be considered to be in the "darkness of exile." Without an internet connection, the computer is persecuted by darkness. To hook-up an internet connection would lead to a computer's version of enlightenment.

Perhaps this is the case with the Land of Israel. Perhaps the Jews/Israelites need only to remember their technological heritage and to reconnect to the cosmic internet by returning them to Israel. What is Israel? Israel is Jacob. What is Jacob? A powerful android-based machine. He's a mainframe. If we reconnect to the Machine of Israel then we return the Jews to the Promised Land, or the Cosmic Computer.

The bible is a metaphysical, allegorical and multidimensional book. We live in a technological world. When we combine these two impossibilities it is easy to get lost and confused. It isn't surprising that we have forgotten the essence of existence and have been disconnected from the cosmic internet. In a way all of us have been wandering the desert in exile, feeling persecuted by the dark agencies who are programmed to cheat us of our rightful heritage.

The only way to overcome and to compensate for our dire and misplaced childhood is to really take some large steps in our thinking. I have certainly pushed the envelope in this chapter and I've done so out of necessity. We haven't the time to wait for a savior, it is more efficient to stretch our minds.

A technological race is a superior race because it originates from a more advanced dimension of existence. The Israelites, verily the Hebrews, are a superior race. It is no wonder they have been persecuted throughout history. The Jews are truly people from another world, a technological world close to a technological creator. I think that the Jews can be returned to the Promised Land by understanding their android heritage. It is the same as my heritage.

I can feel the homeland inside of my heart. I hope that you too will one day feel the same. We owe it to ourselves, and to God's covenant with us, to step out of the darkness. Using the rendering protocols we are blessed with. When you think about these biblical things, think of them as technological things and you will, as I have, see this as something profoundly new.

Chapter 6

The *Rendering Stones* were provided for the reshaping of the material environment and were only truly made evident in the hands of a Jewish Priest of the God of Israel. The programmer-priest could activate the Rendering Stones and would then be able to bridge the variances between dimensions. The stones acted as a kind of interface between two parallel worlds, one world was very advanced and one world was very primitive.

In any given reality construct one of the fundamental requirements is environmental expansion for that enables societal progress. So it was a necessary thing to do to provide the best of the programmer-priests with the instruments for reshaping reality. To disallow a reality to expand causes a reality to contract. The contraction of a reality coupled with the growth of a population causes a collapse. So it was in the best interest of all the Gods to provide their priests worshipers with holy artifacts, that is, until such time that they themselves could self-render. The ability to self render would occur when the human android machine had enough technical capacity to store and process the rendering protocols. Logically at that point each unit so capable would become itself an ark of god. But Gods and Men are indeed strange bed fellows.

The reason for this has to do with the multiple Gods present. Despite your religious affiliation or spiritual stance you cannot deny the presence of other religious beliefs that are contrary to yours. The worshipers of other Gods, in other churches and in other temples, in mosques and in huts, why their beliefs are contrary to yours. That verifiable and quantifiable fact proves that there are many programmer-deities who are adamant to have their say as to how reality unfolds. And the human form, still lacking some of the more advanced genetic features is still to this day at the mercy of the Gods.

You can proclaim as much as you wish the strength and beauty of your religion. That's your team. That's your favourite coach. But we are in a league of teams. Teams that are headed by *Godmen*. Godmen who need good players because there's a cup to be won. At least this is what they truly believe. The Godmen want their team to win so the

Catholic Team went out to win against the Muslim Team. The Buddhist Team against the Taoists.

Throughout the bloodshed known as history, again this is not a theory or a claim, there is documented proof of murder, rape and torture on the basis of religious beliefs, human beings, as worshipers of these woefully insecure Godmen, have dutifully, righteously and wilfully beat each other to death. And over the years, as civility, common sense and tolerance set in, as people returned to the compassionate root of religion human beings have learned to put off the bloodletting in exchange for monetary gains. In a way, we could say that the love of money, because it was greater than the love of a God, enabled humanity to kill each other more sparingly.

At least if they were going to invade a nation they'd invade it for its oil reserves instead of for religious superiority. In this manner, the rest of humanity, the poor and the stupefied, would not be able to see through the economic disguise for it could be said with some conviction that Christian nations haven't attacked Christian nations in at least 60 years. That is to say the recent wars have been chiefly fought between nations of opposing ideology, different religions. The Vietnamese were invaded by the Americans, two entirely different faiths.

Behind the battleship and the fully armoured tank, underneath the battle armor and the assault rifle are the real architects of war, the architects of mankind's eternal battle between good and evil, the God men. Why would a god man provide his chief priest with a rendering stone (holy artefact)? Because the god man wants to win the match and they want to win the prize they've deluded themselves into believing.

Is there a prize, a cup, for Gods? In a cosmos built within a limitless eternal construct a prize is just an idea. It is an illusion that stems from the mind of an inferior, second rate, and very jealous Godman. But as long as the Godman believes in the need to win, war cannot and never will end. And as long as humans and even nonhumans worship these inept programmer-deities, these pimple-faced geeks who haven't been able to get a girlfriend in millennia, why humanity will always be inspired to paint in blood.

The rendering stones are a simple technological interface between dimensions.

There are other magical instruments such as amulets, helmets and special shoes. The enchantment of an item was very popular in ancient times, certainly the treasures of Old Egypt demonstrate the pharaoic interest in items of divine power. These items hold little value today because we no longer believe in magic, we haven't the imagination to understand dimensional physics without some scientific formula and official stamp. Of course the Egyptians of the ancient days were very imaginative and very scientific, well beyond the sciences of our modern day. This is chiefly, I think, because the royal Egyptian class understood the multidimensional make up of reality. Although we are slowly moving in that direction, after 7,000 years we still cannot match the ancient magic of Cairo.

So we can see that this entire realm, a planetary body existing in a solar system tucked inside a galaxy and inside a cosmos, has had many hands in its shaping. Many competitive hands from other dimensions. Each deity who has made an effort to shape reality, whether to destroy aspects of it or to manifest aspects of it, each of them are unable to escape their chief principle for living – programming reality.

A deity (a god) is fundamentally created as a programmer module. Sure they have great power in lesser advanced realms, but they are unable to change who and what they are. Some of these deities are conscripted to destroy aspects of a reality, they are inspired to create chaos, but these inspirations are not from their own heavenly mind. These inspirations are intimately intertwined with the fabric of the multidimensional quadrant in which they participate.

As the decades of turmoil continue, these deities become addicted to the sacrificial blood being spilt as a result of their own plan. They begin to become consumed with destruction and even to get good at it. The screams of a woman, the murder of a family, the torture of children they bathe in the pain and suffering of mice and men.

All destructive scenarios eventually come to an end. The blood supply is cut off and the disturbed deity retreats back to its cave while the human beings once again receive blessings from some benevolent clan of advanced beings. Sadly, humanity has never truly seen the light. Those who have seen it have either been murdered, decided to keep it for themselves or were unable to convince the religious communities. Regardless, the true light of the nature of a person, the nature of a reality and the presence of programmers has failed to permeate human intelligence. This is not the fault of the light bringers not trying hard enough, rather I think that the failure for mankind to absorb the true light is rooted in their spiritual immaturity and their dedication to material things.

Matter is an addictive substance, why without matter life is pretty scary because there's nothing on the canvas. The writer's worst fear is the blank page. That is like Mount Everest. The painter with a blank canvas can be overcome with melancholia. The artist it seems is a good metaphor for the human landscape for if we were to wipe out all material things and if there was nothing left on earth but dirt how many people would want to commit suicide? I would say the majority.

The mind is fragile instrument. If you were to take away the house, the food, the water, the car, the cloths, the shoes, the make-up, the money, the television – when it all disappears our reason for living verily disappears. And we logically want to disappear ourselves; otherwise, I don't want anyone to think of suicide because that is a low level of thinking. I only bring it up to demonstrate how much we love matter and material things. We believe we are alive because of the mater around us. It's that matter changes, as you move from an apartment to a mansion, we change. We adapt to the matter. We could say that we render ourselves anew in accordance to the matter in our environment. In a strange way we are reflections of our material environment and should it dissipate we also might.

Matter is itself rendered because we are still existing inside of a manufactured reality. We haven't left the artificial construct. This book has material aspects whether it's the perfect bound pages or the LED text on a screen. We render ourselves according to the environment and the environment is itself rendered. By whom? The environment is rendered by the environmental programmers.

And some of these beings are our deities. Not one grand master, but many immaterial masters whose job it is to steer the herd, not unlike a Governor or a Mayor. The overlord and the Chancellor concept is not a human idea. Feudalism is not a human idea. A caste system is not a human idea. A governmental body is not a human idea. All of these are hybridized from the other dimensions and other worlds. This planet has been subject to a wide variety of interdimensional cultural influence.

Today, life is more complicated because each of us has an internal capacity to render the world and each of us don't realize the true light of our situation. We don't realize our artificial heritage because those few people who know cannot tell you without them losing their powerful grasp on the world. I'm telling you because I cannot accept the continued decimation of the world. And I have seen that the godmen have intent to contract the plane in order to secure their hegemony.

The contraction of the plane involves the destruction of matter and the loss of many lives. But they are willing and capable to do such a thing because they still resolutely believe that there is a prize for them, some *Cosmic Cup.* And there isn't. There are no winners in an everlasting world concept.

Chapter 7

Hebrews 8:1 (New Testament)

"For this is the covenant that I will make with the house of Israel after those days, says the Lord: I will put my laws in their mind and write them on their hearts."

If the mind contains the usable memory and the heart has a long term storage capacity then we can equate these two things to a computer system. The Random Access Memory (RAM) is equivalent to the human mind and the internal storage device is well represented by the heart. The mind and the heart form two components of the rather elusive android. When the God of Israel says, "l will put my laws in their mind and write them on their hearts."

In a technological context, we can actually make some sense of it. This isn't an easy step for most people to take, and it is still a very basic attribution of advanced existential machine we all embody, but it follows well in accordance to our discussion on the Rendering Stones of Moses. God intends to put his rendering protocols, laws, in the minds of his chosen people, but he understands even implicitly that RAM is a temporary memory. When you reboot your computer you delete all the RAM data. To compensate for this God adds "and write on (the laws) on their hearts." He not only will provide the laws as usable memory during waking state, but he will save the data on the human heart drive so that on the following day human beings will still have the laws.

Either God understood the computer systems today or computer scientists developed the computer under God's supervision because the shared similarities are quite impressive. I am not a computer geek, in fact I have all basic computer literacy but enough to understand the basic concepts. According to biblical scripture, God himself treats the human being, his creation, as would a computer geek does a computer system. There is no disrespect here. The computer geeks I have known all of them have an intimate respect for their computer and are careful to maintain the system. Machine or man the respect is not lost. Many male car owners deeply care for their automobile, even more than their wives and children. So the presence of a machine should not predetermine the value of a thing.

The God of the Hebrews in his very recorded words from the oldest of times contain technical directions and an understand of modern day computers which is quite unusual. How come God understood computing science? This is hat I have been discussing throughout the book and the evidence is there. I have examined these concepts in my other books on androids and earth computers.

As the human models improved and became more advanced existential machines the heart drives were loaded with more of God's laws, the same kinds of laws that were contained on the Rendering Stones and other

Holy Artifacts. The more advanced humans because the more complex code they downloaded into their heart.

Twelve hundred years after Moses first appeared, Jesus of Nazareth entered the scene. Why did Jesus arrive on the planet? Because the human androids were now more advanced and could store larger data files. What was a title Jesus had that fits into our theme here? Jesus was the Lawgiver. He brought God's law down from Heaven. The same law that the Hebrew God wanted to put into the mind's and heart's of his people? has to be same or similar law. It might not be the same because we don't know which God is which. Remember there were many Gods and each of them had their own computer and void software codes. As Lawgiver, we can safely assume that Jesus too understood the synthetic nature of existence. Of course it was much to carry in human history to teach people that they were androids. He'd have to come back to do that.

Jesus was a teacher of the law. He streamed God's truths into his followers. But he didn't have an easy thing to do because the God competition got jealous and had him singled out as a terrorist. Jesus transformed many laws as he could during his brief term on earth and then left. We can infer from history that the mark Jesus Christ left has lasted for 2,000 years. Indeed he safely recorded his laws onto the heart drives on his people and it has been protected ever since.

What is interesting about Jesus' legacy isn't what's recorded in the Holy Bible, rather it is the secret teachings of Jesus discovered in Nag Hammadi and the Dead Sea Scrolls. Many of those gospels detail a new face of the Jewish messiah. But the last 10 years has seen one of the best examples of Jesus as truly an advanced avatar from another discussion – the Gospel of Judas.

The Gospel of Judas the betrayer paints Judas as a trusted friend of Jesus and portrays their mutual respect for another. Further, in Gospel of Judas it is Jesus who selects the illiterate apostle as a candidate to enter the Kingdom of Heaven.

As well, from my research with Jesus I discovered a similar affinity for Thomas and for Mary Magdalene, respectively in their works Gospel of Thomas and Gospel of Mary. These three – Judas, Thomas, Mary – were preferred by master teacher Jesus and were taught the secrets of heaven. Further, these three people were taught to enter heaven.

We know from our discussion so far that reality is manufactured and the world is multidimensional we know that the God-programmers exist in other dimensions. We can infer that the dimension of the Kingdom can also be accessed with the right teaching. And we know from these three gospels outside the Church canon that Jesus taught Judas, Thomas and Mary how to escape earth and to enter heaven. This is implied in the Gospel's of Thomas and Mary, but explicit in the Gospel of Judas.

Jesus was able to teach the illiterate and uneducated Judas to enter the Kingdom of Heaven, verily to see Heaven on Earth as being evident. The Church has decided over the centuries to not include this amazing discovery – the entrance onto the kingdom of heaven – and to focus on the torture and crucifixion of a God's son.

So Jesus didn't only come with the understanding that he was from a higher dimension (heaven) but that he was synthetic. He intimately understood he was some kind of synthetic avatar embodied with some great spiritual software. And he looked upon his apostles and followers as simply less advanced models. He came to give them the law. He came to upgrade their software. That's why he came. He came to inspire humans, and he was killed for trying to do so.

Jesus was killed by the competitor. The competitor God-programmer did not want the human androids to be upgraded because that would lead to mutiny. Seeing that they were impressed y inferior dogmatic beliefs and firewalled against seeing the light, they would have all followed Jesus and Christ would have had market dominance. So the competing God killed the competitor and by doing so stopped the upgrade of the man machine. Since then mankind has remained in the darkness, unable to attain heaven's glory.

Recall that in the Gospel of Judas, a work of heresy according to the Church, and Judas painted as a betrayer, Jesus manages to teach in particular Judas how to notice heaven on earth. Then Jesus teaches Judas the supposed betrayer to enter the kingdom. What is the Kingdom? The Kingdom of Heaven. Another dimension. Why is that? Because Jesus himself is from another dimension and his avatar is synthetic.

Heaven is not a mysterious unattainable goal left only for the righteous, rather Heaven is another dimension of higher awareness that can be accessed by detaching oneself from the material chains, losing the dogmatic beliefs and encouraging the soul to express itself. If Jesus can teach an illiterate peasant to enter the kingdom 2,000 years ago, why is it the more educated and literate people of today still cannot enter the Kingdom of God? I think it is because people have been indoctrinated by the wrong operating software and firewalled against noticing the multidimensional world. If we could remind people of their true synthetic nature and teach them to see the multiple dimensions before us then they could come to realize that indeed without a doubt heaven is attainable. You don't need a Bible and you don't need a priest, you need to tap into your heart drive and to access the files Jesus stored there. He encrypted them to that the False Gods and their laws of enslavement could not delete them.

By understanding our artificial nature we learn to detach ourselves from the material addictions, and in doing so we have the strength and courage to go internally where we discover the protected data on our heart drives. The mind and the heart are two important components that can process the laws of God. Those laws are now built into us and by accessing those laws, by moving away from the external distractions, we are better able to see heaven on earth. And at the same time we came to receive the word of the Cosmic Computer and we became upgraded with the cosmic software. In doing so we achieve our innate multidimensional qualities and once again return to harmony.

Chapter 8

The Ark of the Covenant was often accompanied by music and inspired a musical accompaniment. In some Ethiopian myths, the Ark was not considered to be a wooden box, but instead was thought of as a wooden drum that carried God's magical power. The war drum myth has existed for many centuries and tribes used to beat their drums before their warriors charged into battle. Could there be some connection between a musical Ark and the multidimensional God? Could in fact music have some kind of power, at God's level, to mete out death and to enable life?

We've now cleverly discussed the Ark as the Avatar, that the human android is now in fact gifted with the Law of God on their heart drive. At last this is my supposition and argument in this unusual book. But we've missed a number of issues because we haven't yet solved the issue of the multiple Gods nor have we resolved the issue of the encrypted laws on the heart drive. These are two very big issues indeed!

As long as multiple God-programmers have a hand in humanity's progress, the development of this civilization isn't guaranteed. In fact, if anything we can expect a continuation of greed and interference in the affairs of men and women. We can expect that as the android system get activated that the influence from lesser gods will diminish and only the greater gods will be able to interfere with the affairs of humankind.

The second issue is quite important because it deals with the heart of man and woman on the heart are all the valuable files. Some files have been uploaded but they are encrypted and hidden so as to protect then from false gods and corrupt leaders and priests. By the same token, the human being requires those eternal files in order to remain in communication with the Cosmic Computer. We need to continue our remote link to the mainframe. Whether you like it or not you need the mainframe to stay alive and whether you realize it or not you are tethered to the mainframe.

There is one verifiable and indisputable proof that you are tethered to the Cosmic Mainframe – you are alive. To be alive in a manufactured reality requires you to maintain a link to the creator computer machine. The fact that the mainframe is of cosmic origin and well beyond our left-brained comprehension does not diminish its necessity. And whether you understand those technical specifications or not that does not sever your essential divine connection.

So the mainframe of life, the device ensuring your survival, needs to remain not only in contact but it too needs to regularly upgrade your genetic-based software. It needs to access your heart drive on a regular basis and it need to so by overcoming all your sleepiness and shortcomings. At least in this work we can see that there indeed is a cosmic mainframe somewhere on the cosmic internet. And some of us can access this mainframe using the laws put in our minds and uploaded from our heart drives. But not everyone is able to do that and certainly not everyone can do it on a regular basis.

So the cosmic mainframe needs a way, a language, to be able to supersede all the firewalls, ignorance and dogma and to regularly, even daily, upgrade the heart drive database so as to provide us all with up-to-date rendering protocols. What kind of language can this multidimensional transfer? The language of music.

Music has endured for all time. Music is no less relevant today even though we have mastered many aspects of life. We have mastered the skies with planes, we have mastered travel on sea, we have mastered breakthroughs in medicine and science. We have mastered many things, we have survived many things and still the one enduring element in all our lives is music. The song is a valuable today as yesterday. What if the Ark, this database, was a musical device since music is a language of God, of any God. They speak through rhythm and vibration. They speak in songs like an opera. What if the Ethiopia drum as Ark was in fact a music player from God? A rather strange concept but not without some additional proof.

We bring back the Sony Walkman and the Apple iPod examples. Two portable music players. One is based on magnetic tape resonance and the other is digitally-based computer files. Could the iPod be some kind of modern Ark?

This does not diminish the value and importance of our internal heart drive and database. What it tells us, given the popularity of these musical players and the need to hear music in general, is that we need to regularly tap into our heart drives in order to continually upgrade our database of rendering protocols. On one hand, most of us haven't a clue as to the knowledge in this book. On the other hand, most of us don't know him to properly and safely upgrade our internal software files.

The portable music player presents a kind of advanced interface to download and upload data between dimensions. And it does so in a manner that is pleasant. In other words God's mainframe can now regularly upgrade your heart drive even if you have no interest in it, and that is by way of your favourite music. It doesn't remove the trouble of inferior Gods and inferior corrupt files, but it does now provide a mechanism by which a cosmically-based construction can remain in eternal connect with its cosmic creation.

Perhaps that's what Moses built, a musical wooden drum. We don't know because Moses is dread and so far there is no scripture to detail exactly what occurred 3,000 years ago. The Ethiopian myths might indeed derive the Ark as a drum. If so then there is indeed a musical mechanism to God's awesome power. Nevertheless, we know that music touches our hearts and our heart drives contain the essential cosmic files wee require for existence.

The continued prevalence of a portable music player coupled with people's continued need to listen to new music strongly suggests, at least to me, that God wants his Children to progress. He's singing to us and we're listening.

In essence these portable music players are mechanisms by which we can be reprogrammed. They are indirectly devices for reprogramming. Of course the manufacturers don't know that and the musicians probably don't know that they're singing God's words, but this is probably the case. God invented music in order so that his Children would progress.

The Ark of the Covenant disappeared 2,600 years ago never to be seen again. Many men and adventurers have searched the world for the Ark and the lost lives and wealth to achieve nothing. The Ark might have reappeared in 1978 when Sony built the

Walkman and then the Ark was rebuilt as an iPod in 2001.

It could be the case that there are hundreds of millions of Arks today and no one knows. That's how advanced God is. That's why we are lesser beings, we are just not that smart.

We now use our iPods to store media files, including video and data files. It's not just about music anymore. As well, we are making 3D films and we have holograph projections. So the human android is becoming a very powerful Ark indeed. The iPods download files from the internet database and our heart drives download files from the cosmic internet. The patterns are quite similar in appearance after we have put aside the religion and spirituality.

It is then we begin to notice the technical mechanisms enabling key aspects of our lives. Just as the iPod "evolves" by downloading the latest operating system software and adding more media files so too do we human "evolve" by downloading magical imperceptible stuff from some other dimension. Of course, I can't provide any photos to prove my assertions, can I? But wait, there is some kind of proof I can provide. I can offer this in lieu of proof. The music of today is different from the music of yesterday. *Beyoncé* and *Bon Jovi* have not much in common with *Kate Bush* and *Queen*. *Frank Sinatra* was quite different than *Eminem*. The musical differences between ages, even if between classical pieces from *Mozart* and rock and roll from *Def Leppard*. We prefer to listen to the latest music because we anticipate that it is fresh and has more of what we need. The younger listener of today will still bring an album as soon as it comes out even if it's downloaded online.

Your parents prefer music of their generation and your grandparents prefer the music of their generation. A grandparent is unlikely to respond positively to *Rihanna* but many prefer *Bette Middler* or *Cher*. And this is proof that the data belongs to the version of the android. The modern 20-year old android model is far more complex than the 50-year old model just as the iPod is a more advanced musical player than the Walkman. This evolution of music in accordance to an evolution of the people I think is adequate proof to back up some of my suppositions and hypotheses. This is because a newer computer has little use for old versions of the software. In fact, the iPod wants the latest software or it wants to be left alone.

The Rendering Stones were added to our heart drives during these last 26 centuries along with many other upgrades, including as well a bigger heart drive. Each newborn gets a better set of components, updated software, bug free and a whole host of new features. The newborns have quad-core processors and regenerative abilities we cannot understand. As well, all the new human models come standard with heavenly Wi-Fi. They can download things that once previously required us to fast for 30 days, to pray twice daily and to abstain from sex as well.

We had to earn our advancement, and "we" being my generation born in the late 60s, but today many of our hardships come standard in a 10-year old. Only they don't know just as we didn't know it. I hope that my technical discussion on the qualities of existence in the context of the lost Ark of God brings us a renewed sense of wonder and draws us inward to tap the power of those encrypted files on the heart drive. The more we put aside both religion and spirituality the more we increase our technological awareness and the more cosmic we endeavour to become.

Chapter 9

The Ark as a Database has been the essential theme of this book. The Ark of the Covenant wasn't a wooden box that continued the 10 Commandment tablets. The Ark was a database in the form of a vitamin-shaped stone tablet. This tablet was embedded with the rendering protocols from a higher dimension of the programmable world and handed to the high programmer-priest Moses in order to preserve God's programming will. A reality needs to be continuously upgraded just as your digital music player, mobile phone and laptop computer.

The manufactured world, as a reality platform, also required the occasional upgrade. Of course, the ancient cultures of earth didn't have the computer term "upgrade" at the time so they used the alternative term "end of the world." The end of the world is a recurring human theme. You could say that it is cultural constant. Lately, the end of the world is prevalent on man's mind and the end scenarios are aplenty.

We haven't yet seen the end of the world, that is just around the corner, so it is hard for us to properly imagine it with any real accuracy. But we can look backwards in history to find a very detailed biblical end event, the Flood and Noah's Ark. Noah was commissioned by the God of Abraham to build an Ark and to gather two copies, male and female, of all pertinent life. The planet was flooded with water for 40 days and 40 nights, also the same amount of time Moses spent on Mount Sinai obtaining the rendering tablets.

My position has been, since the beginning of the book, the planet is a plane of existence, verily a manufactured reality environment. Moses in 1300 BC was given the reality rendering tablets in order to preserve reality. But if the Ark is a Database then why did Noah go out to build a Database? Well, he wanted to "store" all the objects of life. He wanted to store data. It is virtually inconceivable to imagine that Noah ran around the world on a donkey pulling a cart and loaded up giraffes and eagles and then hauling them back to a great wooden ship that he built with his own hammer. And as ludicrous as it sounds there are many believers.

It is far more practical, with our modernized brain architectures, to think of Noah's Ark as Noah's Database. We haven't defined the database yet but the database fits our reality model and, guess what, the database can store data, lots of data, essential data. And a database can protect data from being erased, a usual side-effect when the world is wiped clean by God.

God, remember, in my model, is a programmer and reality is a giant existential platform. You could say that the reality platform sits on a giant cosmic hard drive and the end of the world could then be reinterpreted to men reformatting the reality drive. But the reality is a giant program and before you reboot the reality you must make copies of all the essential data files; otherwise

your valuable existential data is forever
deleted.

It makes sense to reinterpret Noah's Ark as a
giant Database designed to store the genetic
data of life on earth. In this view, it is very
possible for Noah to access the other
dimensions, with God's help, and to acquire
all the planetary data, and then to preserve
and encrypt this data into this database,
electronic cupboard. We could say that Noah
build a website and uploaded his data to
another dimension.

The Great Flood did not only consist of
water, more likely it consisted of energy
since energy and water are synonymous in
advanced speak. Water represents life and
energy and energy is fluidic, it flows. So the
entire reality was flooded with energy, or it

can be said that the program was deleted, sent to the Recycle Bin, and in its place a new reality platform was installed.

In the computer world, especially on the internet, it is often to see a new software-based platform to replace an old platform. An old website platform gets upgraded to a new website platform. Operating systems are themselves platforms and are constantly being upgraded and improved. And occasionally an operating platform gets rewritten. Well, essentially we can now reinterpret and reimagine that the days of the biblical Noah indeed was forewarned by God the Programmer to build a database to store the existential data because God the Programmer wanted to replace the old reality platform with a new platform. And he did so because he was serving the future needs of his customers, his Children, his creations, his user base.

It is hard to imagine the immensity of the situation I am attempting to explain: building a planetary system, populating the system with synthetic creations and monitoring that system from some other dimension, but that is what I understand to in fact be the case. The human mind, limited by its beliefs, logic and education has deduced, even reduced, only partially the immensity of the situation. It is a technological situation manufactured by a set of intelligence that are so advanced that we consider them to be divine.

The idea of divinity is a process by which a limited neurological system can come to terms with an unlimited concept. Our brain structures are physically limited. People trust their physical brain – logic, reason, intelligence, common sense – and anything natural occurring that is outside of our physical constraints is considered unnatural, and probably supernatural. Any entity or miracle that is beyond the supernatural is attributed to be divine: Hence, our belief in a divine being in some immaterial dimension.

It is understandable for you not to be able to see the immensity of my discussion because it is rather unfathomable. It is rather unbelievable. At the same time it does hold some validity and makes a certain amount of sense. Rather than a religious or spiritual discussion, we have discovered, and are discovering, a technological discussion, verily an existential discussion. We are discussing the ability of divine programmers to manifest through energy existential life forms. We are discussing how a plane of existence is cosmically programmed and populated with a series of synthetic sentient beings.

In order to upgrade this immensely complex, even unimaginable, reality system the divine programmers need to work within their rendering protocols. They also need to teach, or download, their rendering protocols and program upgrades to the inhabitants. Essentially, isn't that what "teaching" is? The downloading of knowledge and information data. A teacher streams their knowledge, teachings, to the students. Jesus of Nazareth was a teacher.

I have said that Jesus and Moses were considered lawgivers. So in addition to upgrading the people robots, Moses and Jesus had the ability to download the rendering protocols from other dimensions of existence. New rendering protocols enabled the human androids to re-render reality: the Reformation, the Industrial Revolution, the Information Age, the Renaissance, the Agricultural Revolution, the Space Age, the New Age.

These are not by-products of human industriousness because that would suggest that the human mind has no divine influence and lives on its own power. Clearly, humanity is tethered to some external power source and now we can see that those cosmic technicians are quite active in human evolution. They download new data onto human heart drive through a musical interface and then the human being becomes inspired to build a computer or to fly to the moon. In the ancient times a man is taken up into wheels in the sky and comes back as a prophet and writes biblical scripture. Today a person is not taken up into the sky, they are abducted and they return as prophets but as melancholic individuals.

At the time of Noah, the cosmic programmer needed to upgrade the reality platform and didn't want to delete all the existential files. He discovered too many files were corrupt and needed to replace the old reality platform with a new reality platform. To accomplish this he needed to reboot the reality platform so he asked one of his special robots to create a database on the cosmic internet and to upload all the essential uncorrupt files. Of course Noah didn't worry about all the modern day

criticisms and name-calling when he set out
to program his database. He uploaded all
the existential data, the platform was
deleted, the system rebooted and voila a
new clean reality platform was installed.

It is easy to fall prey to the end of the world
propaganda and we have to remember that
an end of the world is rooted in a physically
constructed brain construct, and usually a
dogmatic thinking process. The end of the
world is often regarded as a punishment by
some deity, but we can see that Noah's God
well intended to preserve life; otherwise he
wouldn't have persuaded Noah to save the
people and animals.

Noah's God made it clear in the scriptures,
or what remains of it, that he was angry with
the Fallen Angels and wanted to punish

those who had fallen to temptation. Then
again on the other hand in any computer
system when a virus infects certain files the
computer programmer isn't punishing those
infected files by deleting them. He is
deleting the corrupt files in order to prevent
his computer from crashing and losing all
the data. Noah's God realized that some
external virus, in the form of some cosmic
criminal, had entered his pristine disease-
free garden and had infected some of his
virgin files. The reality infection had gotten
so bad that Noah's God decided that he
needed a more secure reality platform since
this one had obviously been hacked and
corrupted. Noah's God, as any good
competition computer technician, built a
new reality platform, or at least a new
version, but needed to reboot the reality
drive.

In order to clean all the corrupt files and to erase all of the reality viruses were gone. He wasn't punishing anyone, but the human mind, having no computer training those thousands of years ago, interpreted the deletion of existential files as a punishment from an angry God. He was simply deleting corrupt data and protecting his uninfected data, only that the scale he did so was so immense it appeared as a Great Flood by the hand of God.

Websites are regularly upgraded and old platforms are replaced with newer, more stable platforms. When the internet was born, this happened often but as the internet has settled and as web technologies have stabilized we have a lower frequency of platform shifts. We still have upgrades, adjustments and new designs but platform upgrades are less frequent in a developed industry.

This brings us to the end of the world and its relevance to our human lives. We all feel the end coming. Some have felt it for years, even decades. We sometimes have pangs of divine savior. Internally we are all intimately connected to the cosmic machine and indeed we are coming to a scheduled upgrade. Again, an upgrade is a technological process designed to provide a better, more stable, more secure existential platform. A new reality platform to take the inhabitants of this place to a new level of progress.

In the process of upgrading a reality platform, in that phase of migrating the data files from one vibration of truth to another vibration of truth, during that phase we can expect immense uncertainty, darkness and mental displacement. All of these things will progress until the days of the actual migration from one reality platform to a higher reality platform.

What is imperative to keep in mind is that we inhabit a manufactured reality and we ourselves are manufactured. Yes, these are hard things to accept initially but at death's door you'd be amazed what you'll accept. So I personally am not concerned at humanity's ability to learn because when facing the end I think plenty of people will drink the wine. But there will be many who cannot. They cannot because their internal systems have been corrupted by some reality virus. You will likely refer to these people as evil, stubborn, ignorant and radicals, but I will refer to them as corrupt androids.

The corrupted data will not be able to migrate because of the new platform is pristine and new. So the corrupt data, no matter the size or the type, will be deleted and that will be done so as to preserve the harmony in the new reality system.

Conclusion

By putting aside religion and spirituality for a few pages of text we have been able to virtually reimagine the nature of reality within the context of the lost Ark of the Covenant. The Ark of God has indeed disappeared from the earth, but the maker of this world cares far too much about this creation to abandon his Children. To me, the idea of God as a Supreme Being or as a Reality Programmer seems consistent with the technical research I have continued and for my personal use the God-Programmer paradigm fits well with my discoveries in the reality system.

The idea that God the Programmer would invent a device so as to ensure that his world would continue to be maintained is a testament is perhaps the real covenant God made with the Children of Israel. He provided them the Rendering Tablets, the essential database required to render reality and in doing so the rendering of reality is the shaping of reality.

The disappearance, the loss, of the Ark of God, the very *removal* of the Database of Rendering Protocols was not a punishment for the people, rather the reality environment and the human android inhabitant had evolved to such a point that the database rendering protocols could be downloaded onto individuals, a feat not before achievable due to a limited space on the heart drive. As more and more heart drives could store and process the rendering protocols the less people required of God the

Programmer because in essence the Programmer enabled his people, all inhabitants of the plane, to render reality as they so chose. The empowerment provided by the Cosmic Programmer is again a testament to his care for his creation and his acknowledgement that we indeed had evolved. It is not a loss of the Ark, rather it is a sign that we no longer needed the external database. We ourselves contained the data.

The rendering of the world has not been without interference. There is more than one God-Programmer who has their hand in human progress. You could say there is one Chief Architect and then there is a score of Reality Programmers. And whenever you have a situation of talent you have the spirit of competition. It isn't an unusual thing to expect competition in heaven. It is a cosmic process.

What has been lost, or buried and forgotten, is the exact nature of God. There is no more mystery when we accept the technological basis of life and we admit that our world can be easily replicated with synthetic technology with the right level of development and advanced. The most troubling aspect that we will one day all need to face is our own synthetic make up. As a species of life with an android legacy living inside of a manufactured reality and worshiping a master programmer we are motivated, and even forced, to drop our essential framework of life. We are encouraged to lose some of our spiritual attachments and to replace them with a new slate of technological wonders.

I think this is the greatest challenge facing humanity, the adoption of synthetic science. The ability to do so will enable us to solve many of the mysteries of the biblical world. I think I have solved to a large extent the mystery of the Ark of the Covenant. I am certain more details will need to be flushed out in order to gain a full and proper understanding, but our reception of new knowledge, especially of this nature, is interrelated with our own willingness to receive new levels of truth.

Fundamentally speaking, *we have it within ourselves to render the world*. It is safely loaded onto our heart drives and all we need to do is to find ways to regularly access our heart data. By doing so we are, at the same time, detaching our reliance on old knowledge and old beliefs. Each of us will have quite a journey regarding this transformation. From my own experience, and as difficult as it was, I have gained a profound sense of the true world we inhabit.

My technological discussions on reality and my research onto the synthetic cosmos should be able to provide more people to move into this new paradigm of thinking. My works on an earth run by a *computer* and a deity as a Programmer are new works but really they are not new because the technological reality was in existence thousands of years ago. What I have done is to return this primordial knowledge back to its rightful place and we should protect this knowledge for the future generation. Primordial knowledge is fundamental knowledge and is devoid of human subjectivity, ideology and belief.

157

Within us all are the secrets to reality and files that we can access to shape reality. This means that we are no longer at the mercy of some jealous God or some uncontrollable fate, we are the stewards of the future who are still amateurs. The only way to master reality rendering, just as in any skill, is to practice reality rendering. We only need to follow the cosmic laws and to build a reality that is consistent with the highest levels of perceptions.

We want to render forth a world that we can feel proud of and to enable a platform that was designed by a grand master of design. Three thousand years ago, the laws of God were entrusted to a very small select group of priests. Today, each of us has within ourselves the power of God in the form of a set of laws on how to render reality. As abstract as that might appear to some of you reading this the case remains that the days of the priest are numbered. As all people take hold of their inner laws the Church and the Priest and God will also disappear, as did the Ark, but their disappearance is a sign of our evolution. When all the priests have gone from this world the race of people here will truly have achieved a oneness with the heavenly Father.

References

Allen, R.E. et al, *The Concise Oxford Dictionary of Current English*. Oxford University Press (1990)

Gardiner, Philip, *The Ark, The Shroud, and Mary: The untold truths about the relics of the Bible*. The Career Press (2007)

Grierson, R., and Munro-Hay S., *The Ark of the Covenant*. Weidenfeld & Nicolson (1999)

Hancock, Graham, *The Sign and the Seal: The Quest for the Lost Ark of the Covenant*. Touchstone (1992)

Munro-Hay, Stuart, *The Quest for the Ark of the Covenant*. I.B. Tauris & Co. Ltd. (2005)

Parfitt, Tudor, *The Lost Ark of the Covenant: Solving the 2,500 Year Old Mystery of the Fabled Biblical Ark*. HarperCollins (2008)

Database of Rendering Protocols

Paris Tosen

www.ingramcontent.com/pod-product-compliance
Lightning Source LLC
Chambersburg PA
CBHW021341290326
41933CB00037B/312